Transformed

Amber Thompson

Introduction

Have you ever had an encounter with the Holy Spirit that is so profound you cannot ignore it? Not long after receiving a wake-up call regarding my health, I had an amazing, life-changing moment that inspired me to bravely submit fully to God's will. I recall sitting in a chair in the front room of the house where I was residing at the time. There was a holiday party taking place, the house was beautifully decorated, lots of delicious treats being served, and a distinct Christmas tune played in the background. I vividly recall being in an extremely dark, desperate, lonely space in my life and recognizing that significant changes had to be made. I was morbidly obese, emotionally wrecked, and out of lies to cover it all up. I typically do not aspire to New Year's resolutions because, let's be honest, after the proverbial "ball" drops, WE drop the ball (on ourselves) and nothing gets resolved. However, in that moment, my thoughts began to change. I came up with hashtag revitalization (#revitalization). I had a desire to alter my mind, body, and spirit going into the new year.

To undergo a transformation is an elective process. It is a choice to bravely address all the dark corners that have kept us consistently inconsistent, visibly invisible, and no longer content with being content. The decision to change the current of my life required some of my toughest days, but there was abundant joy after the struggle. By giving everything back to God, His power has phenomenal voltage as he uses us to light up his Kingdom. Meriam -Webster defines transform: to make a thorough or dramatic change in form, appearance, or character of your life. Just like the size of this book, it only takes one small, yet courageous step towards the Father for your future to be transformed. I hope the words within these pages encourage and inspire as the precious hand of God lovingly transforms you, and a divine metamorphosis occurs in your life. Romans 12:2

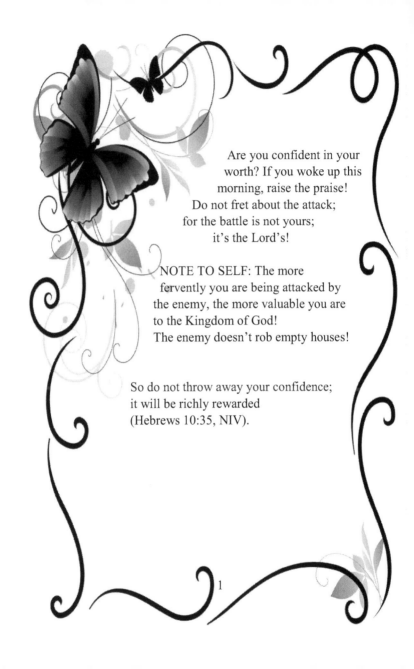

Are you confident in your
worth? If you woke up this
morning, raise the praise!
Do not fret about the attack;
for the battle is not yours;
it's the Lord's!

NOTE TO SELF: The more
fervently you are being attacked by
the enemy, the more valuable you are
to the Kingdom of God!
The enemy doesn't rob empty houses!

So do not throw away your confidence;
it will be richly rewarded
(Hebrews 10:35, NIV).

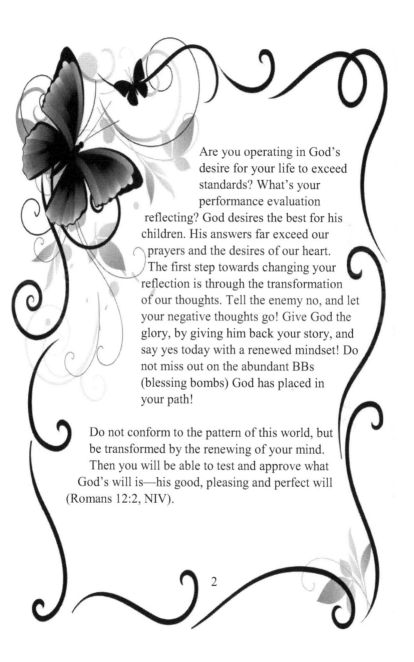

Are you operating in God's desire for your life to exceed standards? What's your performance evaluation reflecting? God desires the best for his children. His answers far exceed our prayers and the desires of our heart. The first step towards changing your reflection is through the transformation of our thoughts. Tell the enemy no, and let your negative thoughts go! Give God the glory, by giving him back your story, and say yes today with a renewed mindset! Do not miss out on the abundant BBs (blessing bombs) God has placed in your path!

Do not conform to the pattern of this world, but be transformed by the renewing of your mind. Then you will be able to test and approve what God's will is—his good, pleasing and perfect will (Romans 12:2, NIV).

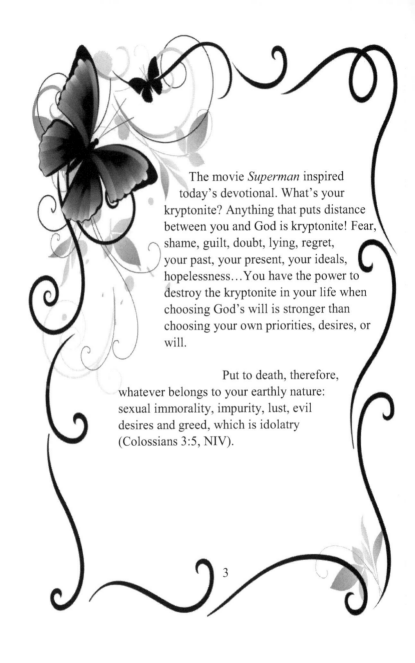

The movie *Superman* inspired today's devotional. What's your kryptonite? Anything that puts distance between you and God is kryptonite! Fear, shame, guilt, doubt, lying, regret, your past, your present, your ideals, hopelessness…You have the power to destroy the kryptonite in your life when choosing God's will is stronger than choosing your own priorities, desires, or will.

Put to death, therefore, whatever belongs to your earthly nature: sexual immorality, impurity, lust, evil desires and greed, which is idolatry (Colossians 3:5, NIV).

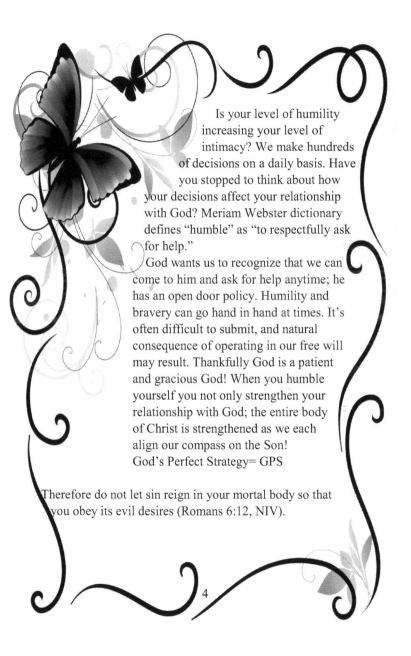

Is your level of humility increasing your level of intimacy? We make hundreds of decisions on a daily basis. Have you stopped to think about how your decisions affect your relationship with God? Meriam Webster dictionary defines "humble" as "to respectfully ask for help."

God wants us to recognize that we can come to him and ask for help anytime; he has an open door policy. Humility and bravery can go hand in hand at times. It's often difficult to submit, and natural consequence of operating in our free will may result. Thankfully God is a patient and gracious God! When you humble yourself you not only strengthen your relationship with God; the entire body of Christ is strengthened as we each align our compass on the Son! God's Perfect Strategy= GPS

Therefore do not let sin reign in your mortal body so that you obey its evil desires (Romans 6:12, NIV).

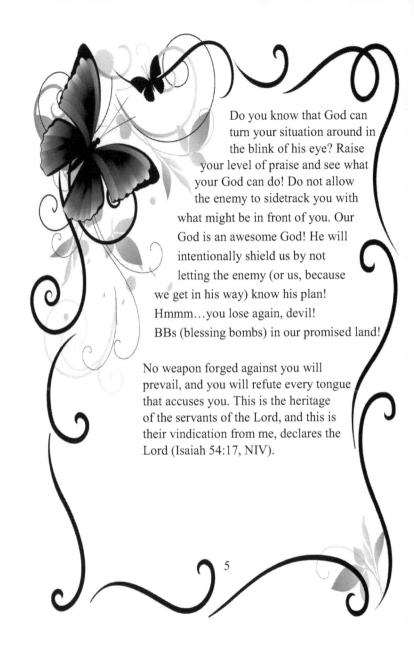

Do you know that God can turn your situation around in the blink of his eye? Raise your level of praise and see what your God can do! Do not allow the enemy to sidetrack you with what might be in front of you. Our God is an awesome God! He will intentionally shield us by not letting the enemy (or us, because we get in his way) know his plan! Hmmm…you lose again, devil! BBs (blessing bombs) in our promised land!

No weapon forged against you will prevail, and you will refute every tongue that accuses you. This is the heritage of the servants of the Lord, and this is their vindication from me, declares the Lord (Isaiah 54:17, NIV).

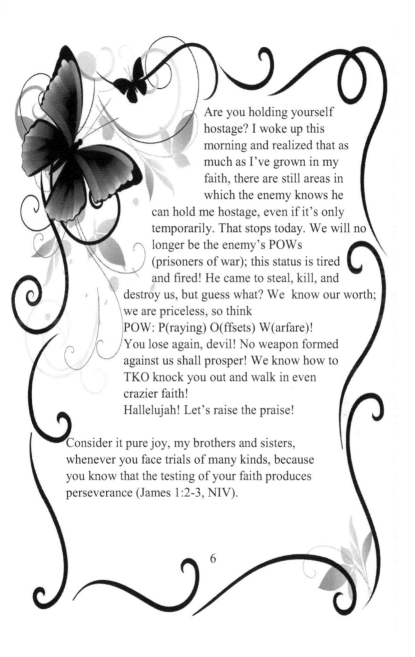

Are you holding yourself hostage? I woke up this morning and realized that as much as I've grown in my faith, there are still areas in which the enemy knows he can hold me hostage, even if it's only temporarily. That stops today. We will no longer be the enemy's POWs (prisoners of war); this status is tired and fired! He came to steal, kill, and destroy us, but guess what? We know our worth; we are priceless, so think POW: P(raying) O(ffsets) W(arfare)! You lose again, devil! No weapon formed against us shall prosper! We know how to TKO knock you out and walk in even crazier faith!
Hallelujah! Let's raise the praise!

Consider it pure joy, my brothers and sisters, whenever you face trials of many kinds, because you know that the testing of your faith produces perseverance (James 1:2-3, NIV).

Are we there yet, God? "Eyes have not seen and ears have not heard all the wonderful things God has prepared for us."

Be encouraged; God has dispatched angels to go ahead and prepare the way for us. Stop rushing God's perfect timing; trust his process and promises! Next stop… divine destination!

We must pay the most careful attention, therefore, to what we have heard, so that we do not drift away (Hebrews 2:1 NIV)

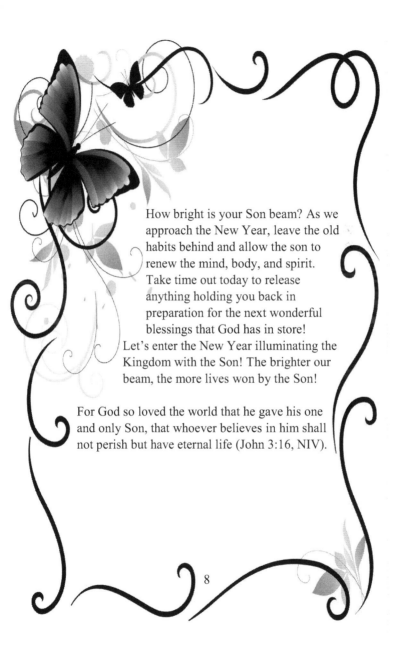

How bright is your Son beam? As we approach the New Year, leave the old habits behind and allow the son to renew the mind, body, and spirit. Take time out today to release anything holding you back in preparation for the next wonderful blessings that God has in store! Let's enter the New Year illuminating the Kingdom with the Son! The brighter our beam, the more lives won by the Son!

For God so loved the world that he gave his one and only Son, that whoever believes in him shall not perish but have eternal life (John 3:16, NIV).

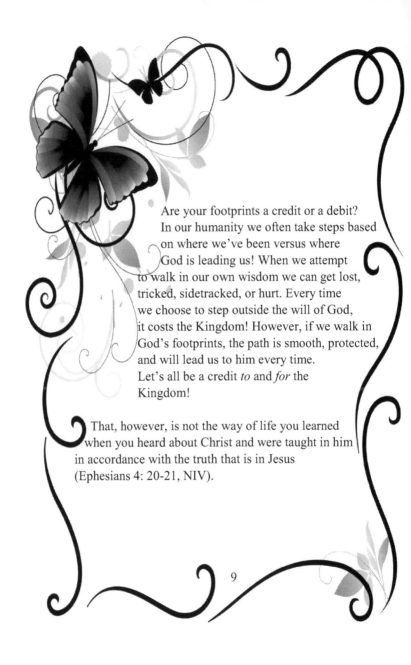

Are your footprints a credit or a debit?
In our humanity we often take steps based
on where we've been versus where
God is leading us! When we attempt
to walk in our own wisdom we can get lost,
tricked, sidetracked, or hurt. Every time
we choose to step outside the will of God,
it costs the Kingdom! However, if we walk in
God's footprints, the path is smooth, protected,
and will lead us to him every time.
Let's all be a credit *to* and *for* the
Kingdom!

That, however, is not the way of life you learned
when you heard about Christ and were taught in him
in accordance with the truth that is in Jesus
(Ephesians 4: 20-21, NIV).

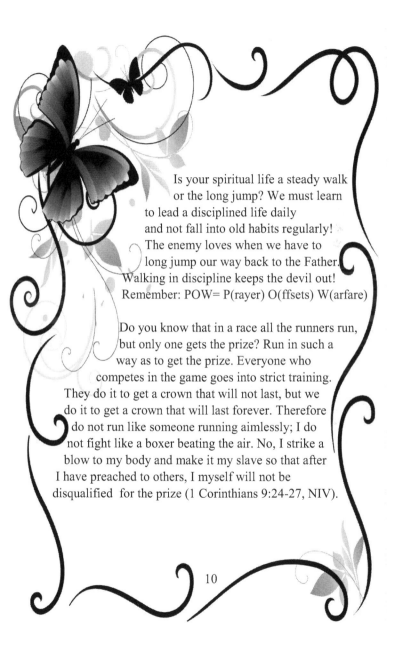

Is your spiritual life a steady walk
or the long jump? We must learn
to lead a disciplined life daily
and not fall into old habits regularly!
The enemy loves when we have to
long jump our way back to the Father.
Walking in discipline keeps the devil out!
Remember: POW= P(rayer) O(ffsets) W(arfare)

Do you know that in a race all the runners run,
but only one gets the prize? Run in such a
way as to get the prize. Everyone who
competes in the game goes into strict training.
They do it to get a crown that will not last, but we
do it to get a crown that will last forever. Therefore
do not run like someone running aimlessly; I do
not fight like a boxer beating the air. No, I strike a
blow to my body and make it my slave so that after
I have preached to others, I myself will not be
disqualified for the prize (1 Corinthians 9:24-27, NIV).

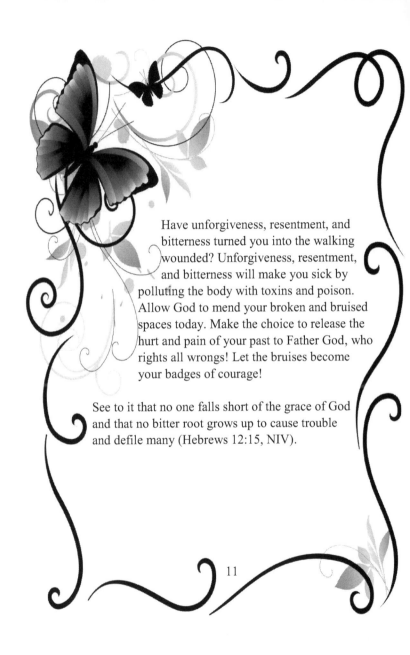

Have unforgiveness, resentment, and bitterness turned you into the walking wounded? Unforgiveness, resentment, and bitterness will make you sick by polluting the body with toxins and poison. Allow God to mend your broken and bruised spaces today. Make the choice to release the hurt and pain of your past to Father God, who rights all wrongs! Let the bruises become your badges of courage!

See to it that no one falls short of the grace of God and that no bitter root grows up to cause trouble and defile many (Hebrews 12:15, NIV).

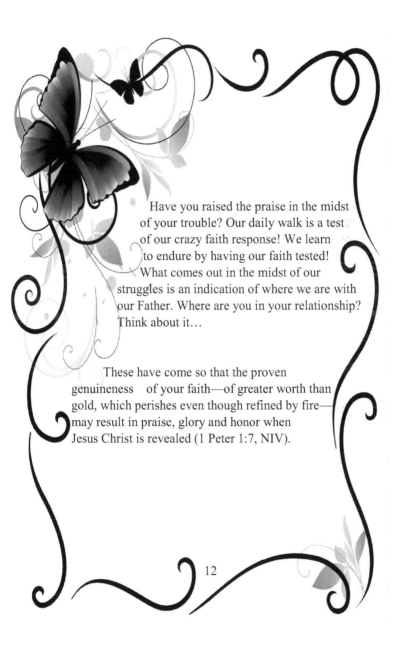

Have you raised the praise in the midst of your trouble? Our daily walk is a test of our crazy faith response! We learn to endure by having our faith tested! What comes out in the midst of our struggles is an indication of where we are with our Father. Where are you in your relationship? Think about it…

These have come so that the proven genuineness of your faith—of greater worth than gold, which perishes even though refined by fire—may result in praise, glory and honor when Jesus Christ is revealed (1 Peter 1:7, NIV).

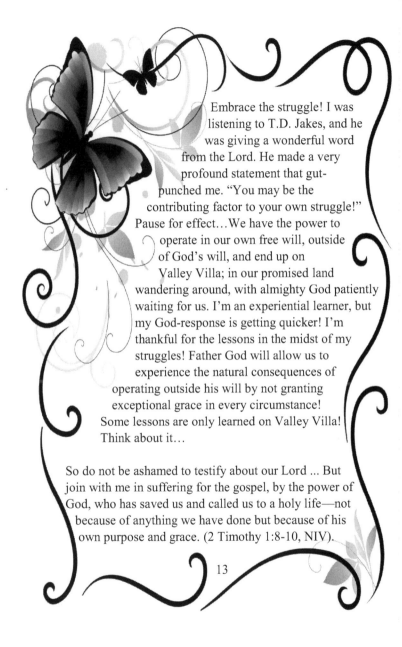

Embrace the struggle! I was listening to T.D. Jakes, and he was giving a wonderful word from the Lord. He made a very profound statement that gut-punched me. "You may be the contributing factor to your own struggle!" Pause for effect…We have the power to operate in our own free will, outside of God's will, and end up on Valley Villa; in our promised land wandering around, with almighty God patiently waiting for us. I'm an experiential learner, but my God-response is getting quicker! I'm thankful for the lessons in the midst of my struggles! Father God will allow us to experience the natural consequences of operating outside his will by not granting exceptional grace in every circumstance! Some lessons are only learned on Valley Villa! Think about it…

So do not be ashamed to testify about our Lord … But join with me in suffering for the gospel, by the power of God, who has saved us and called us to a holy life—not because of anything we have done but because of his own purpose and grace. (2 Timothy 1:8-10, NIV).

13

Have you given everything to God? attended church last night and made the decision to have my tithes automatically withdrawn from my paycheck, giving God complete power over his money. I'm not making this declaration for accolades. I'm sharing for the purpose of giving God everything in every area of our lives to expand his territory. How can we expect to be rulers over many if we cannot be trusted with the simple commands?

Bring the whole title into the storehouse, that there may be food in my house. Test me in this, says the Lord Almighty, and see if I will not throw open the floodgates of heaven and pour out so much blessing that there will not be room enough to store it (Malachi 3:10, NIV).

14

Have you ever rushed in when you should have backed off? I work daily on my relationships and godly conflict resolution. Thank you, Lord, for deliverance from the spirit of needing to have the last word! Sometimes our reason is one of the following: we don't feel qualified, so we strive to seem superior; we want to remain relevant, constantly seeking approval from others; our voice has never been acknowledged; we simply desire to be heard; we've been invisible our whole life; we lack self-confidence; lack of respect for ourselves or others; we're selfish, self- centered; we want to be remembered; and the list goes on...

Ouch! Thank you, Lord, that you *zacar* (Hebrew word for remember) us. We will no longer be fools who rush in; you are there in the midst working things out in our favor.

"It is to one's honor to avoid strife, but every fool is quick to quarrel (Proverbs 20:3, NIV)."

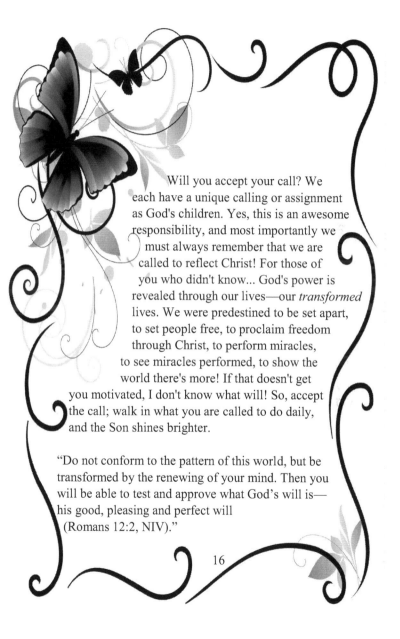

Will you accept your call? We each have a unique calling or assignment as God's children. Yes, this is an awesome responsibility, and most importantly we must always remember that we are called to reflect Christ! For those of you who didn't know... God's power is revealed through our lives—our *transformed* lives. We were predestined to be set apart, to set people free, to proclaim freedom through Christ, to perform miracles, to see miracles performed, to show the world there's more! If that doesn't get you motivated, I don't know what will! So, accept the call; walk in what you are called to do daily, and the Son shines brighter.

"Do not conform to the pattern of this world, but be transformed by the renewing of your mind. Then you will be able to test and approve what God's will is— his good, pleasing and perfect will (Romans 12:2, NIV)."

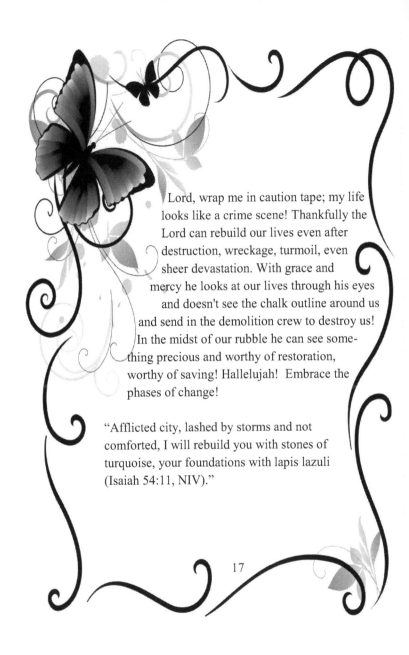

Lord, wrap me in caution tape; my life looks like a crime scene! Thankfully the Lord can rebuild our lives even after destruction, wreckage, turmoil, even sheer devastation. With grace and mercy he looks at our lives through his eyes and doesn't see the chalk outline around us and send in the demolition crew to destroy us! In the midst of our rubble he can see something precious and worthy of restoration, worthy of saving! Hallelujah! Embrace the phases of change!

"Afflicted city, lashed by storms and not comforted, I will rebuild you with stones of turquoise, your foundations with lapis lazuli (Isaiah 54:11, NIV)."

17

Our mouth matters!
The spoken word holds power...
power to break chains,
cast out evil/things that are not of
God, heal the sick, lead someone to Christ,
build up and affirm, speak about the
miracles you've seen, inspire, even
lead nations. So, how are you using
your mouth? What's coming out of your
mouth is a reflection of what's inside you—
the God in you. Are you all right with the
reflection in your mirror?

"Listen, for I have trustworthy things to say; I
open my lips to speak what is right
(Proverbs 8:6, NIV)."

18

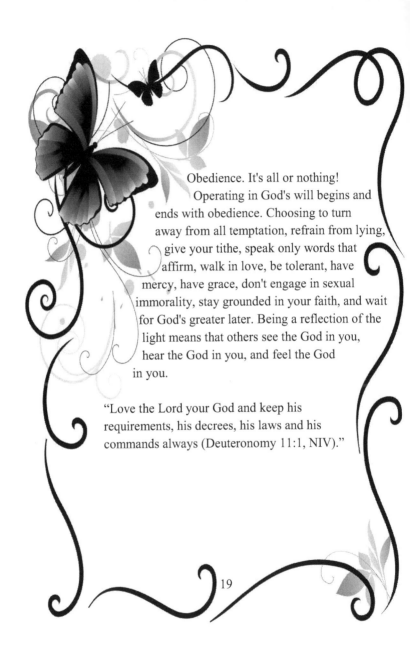

Obedience. It's all or nothing!
Operating in God's will begins and ends with obedience. Choosing to turn away from all temptation, refrain from lying, give your tithe, speak only words that affirm, walk in love, be tolerant, have mercy, have grace, don't engage in sexual immorality, stay grounded in your faith, and wait for God's greater later. Being a reflection of the light means that others see the God in you, hear the God in you, and feel the God in you.

"Love the Lord your God and keep his requirements, his decrees, his laws and his commands always (Deuteronomy 11:1, NIV)."

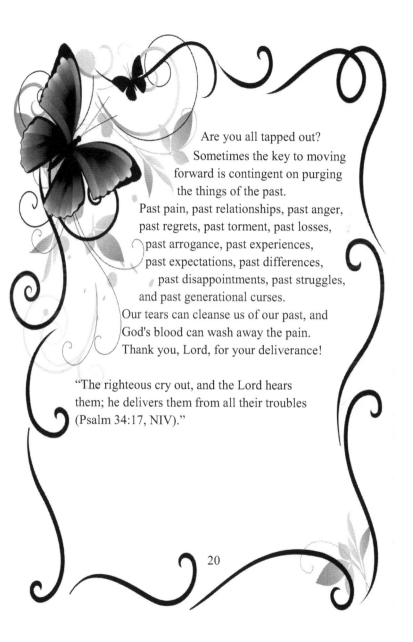

Are you all tapped out?
Sometimes the key to moving
forward is contingent on purging
the things of the past.
Past pain, past relationships, past anger,
past regrets, past torment, past losses,
past arrogance, past experiences,
past expectations, past differences,
past disappointments, past struggles,
and past generational curses.
Our tears can cleanse us of our past, and
God's blood can wash away the pain.
Thank you, Lord, for your deliverance!

"The righteous cry out, and the Lord hears
them; he delivers them from all their troubles
(Psalm 34:17, NIV)."

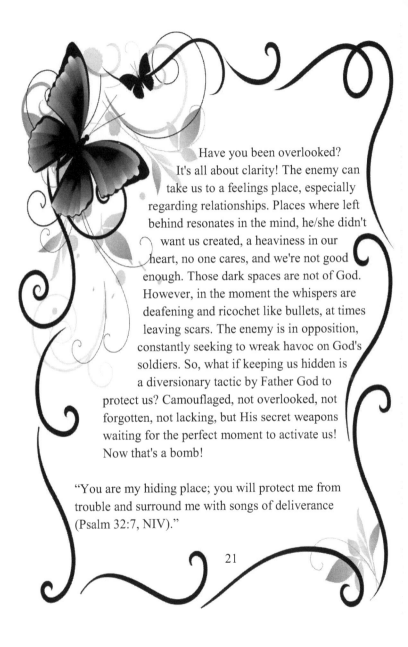

Have you been overlooked? It's all about clarity! The enemy can take us to a feelings place, especially regarding relationships. Places where left behind resonates in the mind, he/she didn't want us created, a heaviness in our heart, no one cares, and we're not good enough. Those dark spaces are not of God. However, in the moment the whispers are deafening and ricochet like bullets, at times leaving scars. The enemy is in opposition, constantly seeking to wreak havoc on God's soldiers. So, what if keeping us hidden is a diversionary tactic by Father God to protect us? Camouflaged, not overlooked, not forgotten, not lacking, but His secret weapons waiting for the perfect moment to activate us! Now that's a bomb!

"You are my hiding place; you will protect me from trouble and surround me with songs of deliverance (Psalm 32:7, NIV)."

21

You can rock this boat, but you can't tip it over! In the midst of the storm, we have crazy faith! Do not be tossed around by the crashing waves of life's circumstances. We may not see it, but the sun is right behind the clouds.

"Now faith is confidence in what we hope for and assurance about what we do not see (Hebrews 11:1, NIV)."

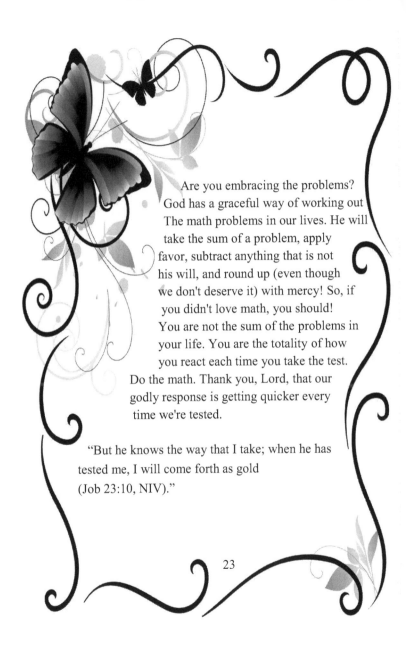

Are you embracing the problems? God has a graceful way of working out the math problems in our lives. He will take the sum of a problem, apply favor, subtract anything that is not his will, and round up (even though we don't deserve it) with mercy! So, if you didn't love math, you should! You are not the sum of the problems in your life. You are the totality of how you react each time you take the test. Do the math. Thank you, Lord, that our godly response is getting quicker every time we're tested.

"But he knows the way that I take; when he has tested me, I will come forth as gold (Job 23:10, NIV)."

No more hiding in the dark! Speaking truth frees us from the darkness holding us back! Say out loud that you lie, cheated, are currently cheating, have no money, failed class in school, have no direction, don't have meaningful relationships with anyone, are unhappy in your marriage, feel disconnected from your faith and God, stopped going to church, eat in the dark, have no identity, feel invisible, struggle with anxiety or depression, aren't confident, are ashamed about the divorce, hate your body, feel alone, complain about everything, are never happy but want to be, desire to be married, are tired of being single, feel tortured by life, want to give up, tried to kill yourself, are contemplating suicide now, or feel defeated. There is nothing too big for Jesus! It's time to let go of the past, grow in Christ, and glow from here! Thank you, Lord, for renewed beginnings!

"Come near to God and he will come near to you. Wash your hands, you sinners, and purify your hearts, you double-minded (James 4:8, NIV)"

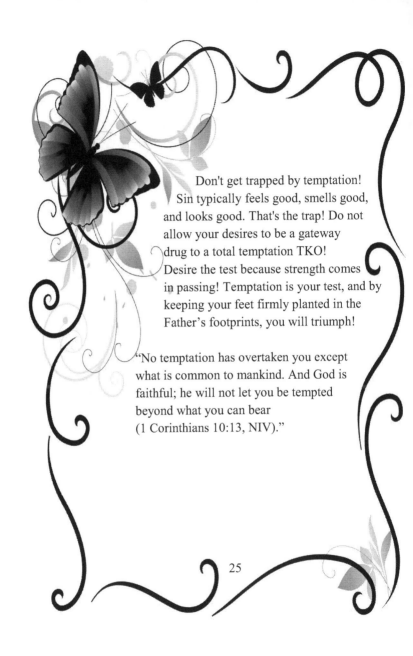

Don't get trapped by temptation! Sin typically feels good, smells good, and looks good. That's the trap! Do not allow your desires to be a gateway drug to a total temptation TKO! Desire the test because strength comes in passing! Temptation is your test, and by keeping your feet firmly planted in the Father's footprints, you will triumph!

"No temptation has overtaken you except what is common to mankind. And God is faithful; he will not let you be tempted beyond what you can bear (1 Corinthians 10:13, NIV)."

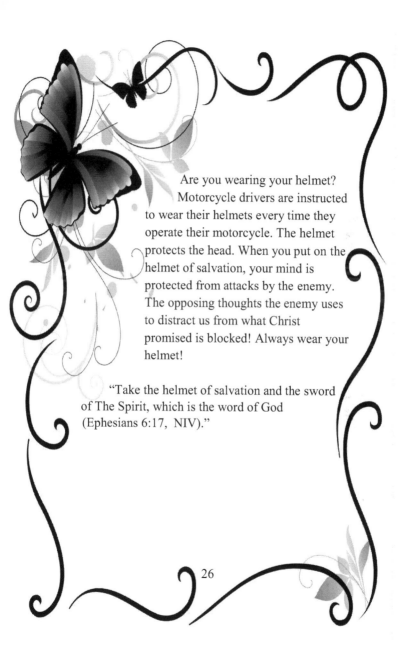

Are you wearing your helmet? Motorcycle drivers are instructed to wear their helmets every time they operate their motorcycle. The helmet protects the head. When you put on the helmet of salvation, your mind is protected from attacks by the enemy. The opposing thoughts the enemy uses to distract us from what Christ promised is blocked! Always wear your helmet!

"Take the helmet of salvation and the sword of The Spirit, which is the word of God (Ephesians 6:17, NIV)."

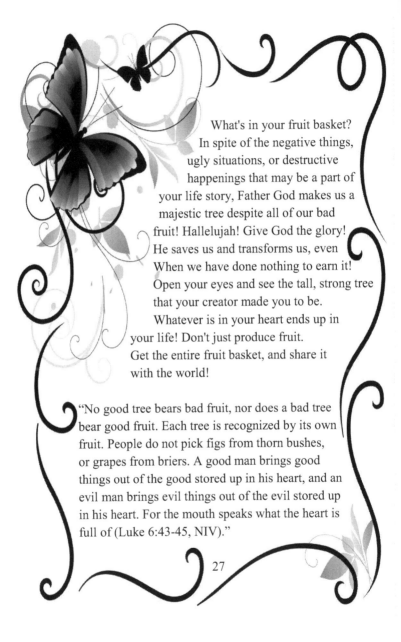

What's in your fruit basket? In spite of the negative things, ugly situations, or destructive happenings that may be a part of your life story, Father God makes us a majestic tree despite all of our bad fruit! Hallelujah! Give God the glory! He saves us and transforms us, even When we have done nothing to earn it! Open your eyes and see the tall, strong tree that your creator made you to be.

Whatever is in your heart ends up in your life! Don't just produce fruit. Get the entire fruit basket, and share it with the world!

"No good tree bears bad fruit, nor does a bad tree bear good fruit. Each tree is recognized by its own fruit. People do not pick figs from thorn bushes, or grapes from briers. A good man brings good things out of the good stored up in his heart, and an evil man brings evil things out of the evil stored up in his heart. For the mouth speaks what the heart is full of (Luke 6:43-45, NIV)."

27

Are you on a Holy Ghost high?
Take a moment to think about how
blessed you are. We can get so distracted
by the trials that we completely miss
the triumphant moments in the midst
of difficulties. Raise the praise in every
situation; bless the Lord at all times!
We serve an all-the-time God, so we
shouldn't have part-time faith! Our God
is a God of favor and glory! Those who
trust in the Lord are truly happy.

"Lord Almighty, blessed is the one who trusts in
you (Psalms 84:12, NIV)."

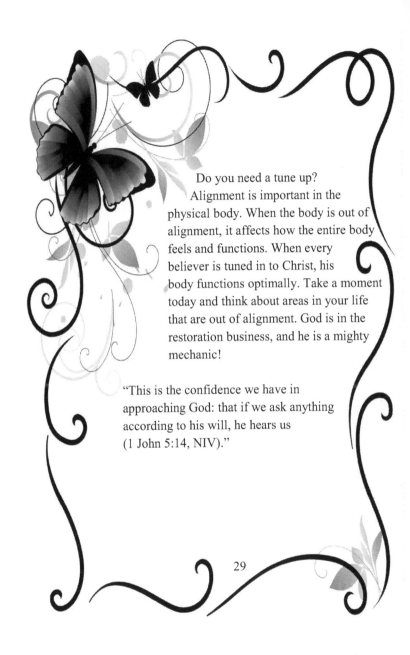

Do you need a tune up?
Alignment is important in the physical body. When the body is out of alignment, it affects how the entire body feels and functions. When every believer is tuned in to Christ, his body functions optimally. Take a moment today and think about areas in your life that are out of alignment. God is in the restoration business, and he is a mighty mechanic!

"This is the confidence we have in approaching God: that if we ask anything according to his will, he hears us (1 John 5:14, NIV)."

What's your problem?

If you are going to walk in your kingdom calling, you are going to face adversity! Recognize that the problem standing in front of your promise is a trap! Do not get tricked! The level of attack by the enemy is a direct correlation to your worth in the kingdom of glory! Thank you, Lord, for the problems!

"Be alert and of sober mind. Your enemy the devil prowls around like a roaring lion looking for someone to devour (1 Peter 5:8, NIV)."

30

Today is the day when you say enough is enough to the old stuff! This time the chains are completely broken; nothing can hold you hostage! The amount of control Christ has in your life equals the amount of freedom in your life! Think about it!

"Now the Lord is the Spirit, and where the Spirit of the Lord is, there is freedom (2 Corinthians 3:17, NIV)."

Made in the USA
Monee, IL
23 December 2023